BRITAIN IN OLD PHOTOGRAPHS

RUGBY & DISTRICT

A SECOND SELECTION

RUGBY LOCAL HISTORY
RESEARCH GROUP

SUTTON PUBLISHING LIMITED

Sutton Publishing Limited
Phoenix Mill · Thrupp · Stroud
Gloucestershire · GL5 2BU

First published 1997

Cover photographs. Front: Lillian Murphy with
rugby balls at Gilbert's workshop; back: children
with a model tram built by Mr Frank Renshaw in
Whitehall Recreation Ground, late 1940s.

British Library Cataloguing in Publication Data
A catalogue record for this book is available from the
British Library.

ISBN 0-7509-1681-8

Typeset in 10/12 Perpetua.
Typesetting and origination by
Sutton Publishing Limited.
Printed in Great Britain by
Ebenezer Baylis, Worcester.

Edward and Ada Truelove pictured with their bicycles at the back of 8 Regents Place, 1926. Edward
Truelove started his agricultural engineering business in August 1914.

CONTENTS

Blue Bells from Rugby

A picture postcard from Rugby showing off some of the local attractions in the early 1900s.

INTRODUCTION

When asked if we, the Rugby Local History Research Group, would like to produce a second book of *Rugby & District in Old Photographs* we were unsure whether or not we would be able to find enough material for it. In the event we need not have worried about this as from the collections of friends, family and other sources we were able to make what we hope is another interesting selection. Some photographs have also been obtained from the Rugby Public Library Collection. The Public Library, originally provided in 1890 by local benefactor R.H. Wood, is finally being replaced with a modern building which will also house a much-needed local museum. A temporary library, with reduced facilities, must be endured for two years but the reward is in sight.

Rugby is famous for its game and rugby footballs are still manufactured here by Gilbert's. This is something of which the town is justly proud and we have made a special feature of their business in this book. Even as this is being written, rugby football features in the local press with the announcement that England and British Lions International, Jeremy Guscott, will unveil the new statue of William Webb Ellis in September 1997. Sport, of all kinds, has always been well supported in the town, and many of the larger local firms had their own sports grounds and facilities for different sporting activities, as can be seen from our photographs.

Transport and movement of goods concern everybody. Recently a new rail freight terminus has been built at Crick, just outside Rugby. It is hoped that this will relieve the pressure of traffic travelling from the Channel ports to the Midlands. The major roads, M1, M6, A14 and A5, are all close by, crossing from north to south and from east to west. A new hourly rail service from Rugby to Gatwick was started in June 1997, an asset for Rugbeians and visitors alike. It is also hoped that the new Eurostar trains will be stopping here, linking us directly to continental Europe. Sadly the old LNER railway line that ran through the town no longer exists, and its cutting is now a well-used nature reserve and trail called Great Central Walk. An attempt was made to re-open the line for freight traffic in 1996 but, facing fierce local opposition, Parliament rejected the proposal.

On a lighter note, the happy faces of children at play are well represented as are local people enjoying themselves in recreation and taking part in amateur dramatics, both plays and musicals. Dr Raymond Owen was instrumental in the formation of the Rugby Theatre Society nearly fifty years ago. The old Scala cinema in Henry Street was acquired and the first production was staged on 5 December 1949: the theatre continues to thrive today. Schooldays, weddings from different periods, town and country buildings and some reminders of wartime are all included. We do hope that we have chosen wisely and that you will enjoy this new selection. Memories begin to dim and photographs fade with age, and in some cases it has been difficult for names and faces to be remembered by the owners of the photographs. However, we hope that any errors which you may find will not spoil your enjoyment.

Mary Aliberti (Group Leader)

Four elderly ladies sit in an open car and face the camera with serious expressions. The date of the picture is not known but the age of the vehicle and the ladies' attire suggests the early 1900s. The ladies were apparently all sisters. One is Mrs Wright, grandmother of Jim Wright from Manor Farm, Monks Kirby. The others, Kate and Alice Truelove and Fannie Hollick, were his great aunts.

GILBERT'S RUGBY
FOOTBALLS

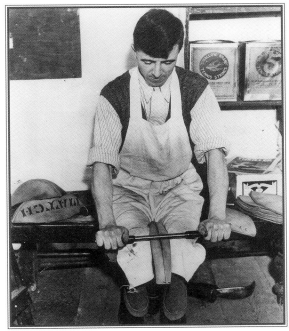

The Gilbert Company was established in the early nineteenth century by William Gilbert, a boot and shoe maker in High Street. It was a short step from repairing the shoes of Rugby School boys to providing leather casings for their footballs. William Webb Ellis very probably had a ball made by William in his arms when he decided to run with it in 1823. From those days 'Match' balls were made for big games at the School and 'Puntabouts' for practice. The business moved to St Matthew's Street in 1842 where rugby footballs have been made ever since. William was followed by James I, James II, James John and then James IV. The company was taken over by Rodney Webb (Newbold, Coventry and England international rugby player), who runs the old shop as a rugby football museum and has re-established the international reputation of the Gilbert ball, now selected once again for the 1999 Rugby Union World Cup.

In the picture on the left James John Gilbert is seen outside his shop in St Matthew's Street, early 1900s. He inherited the business from his father, James II, in 1906 but had already been actively involved for many years. His wife Mary continued to run the business with his son James after James John's death. Featured in the window display is a wide selection of cricket bats and tennis racquets.

In this photograph James John Gilbert is shown standing outside his home at 4 Pennington Street. One of his main interests outside his football-making occupation was playing the game of rugby. He was a member of the Rugby Lions in the early years of the club and broke his collar bone three times while playing.

Alf Archer, one of Gilbert's ball stitchers, hand stretching the damp leather sections of a ball, 1930s. The reason for this was to take as much stretch out of the leather prior to rolling, cutting and stitching the panels.

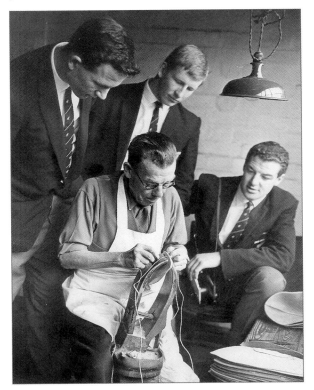

A Gilbert's stitcher at work sewing together the leather panels of a Match rugby football under the rapt gaze of three members of a New Zealand international touring team. Many such posed photographs probably grace the rugby clubhouses of the world, not to mention the homes of the players themselves.

James Gilbert (1885–1967) was the last of the family to run the ball manufacturing business. He is pictured, second from the right, showing members of the New Zealand Rugby Touring Team around the workshops. It was he who had established the tradition of inviting international touring sides to see rugby balls being made.

During the afternoon of Charter Day in 1932 a parade of vehicles and floats, including this one from rugby ball makers Gilbert's, drove through the town. Two stitchers, Jack Rowlett and Sidney Esther, demonstrated ball making surrounded by the finished articles. The claim on the float still holds good today, sixty-five years later.

SPORT & LEISURE

Newbold Tennis Club, pictured here in the 1930s, met regularly and played on a court in a field belonging to the Boughton-Leigh family. It was located opposite St Botolph's Church and backed on to the canal. They played matches against other villages, travelling as far as Woodford Halse. This, like other villages, was easily reached by train on the LNER railway from the Central station. The whole experience was a lot of fun! This photograph includes Jack Gibbs, James Collins, Albert Gamble and Jack Keats. Seated: Donald Gibbs and William Old. Both Jack Gibbs and Jack Keats were killed in the Second World War.

Dorothy and Marjorie Hargrave ready for tennis at Braunston, *c*. 1920. They were the daughters of the village baker, Earnest Albert Hargrave.

Members of the BTH Tennis Club, early 1960s. Open tournaments were held within the club and with other clubs in the Coventry and District Tennis League. David Stewart is sitting in the middle of the front row and his wife Mary is standing in the middle back.

BTH Tennis Club ladies' team, mid-1950s. Two ladies' teams are pictured after winning the Coventry League. Back row, left to right: Mary Stewart, Gladys Faulks, Kath Hewitt, -?-. Front row: Dorothy Terrel, Betty Brown, -?-, Marjorie Beck.

This photo of the BTH Publicity Tennis Group was taken on 9 July 1952 at the Firs in Bilton Road. Standing, left to right: Mr Alderson, T.M. McClellan, Mr Spence, E. Walton, -?-, A. Campbell, Mrs Jones, Tony Hoflin, -?-, -?-, -?-, Mr Bilson, Mr Crumpsty, -?-. Seated: Ros Childs, -?-, Miss Evelyn Hunt, -?-, Joan Clipstone, Hughie Jones, -?-, -?-, Barbara Sparrow, -?-.

On 18 June 1955 the Rugby LMS Tug-o'-War team won their event at the Railway Sports in London. On their return home they posed for the camera with the magnificent shield and their individual trophies. Clem Harrison is second from the left in the front row.

Rugby Central FC, 1929/30 winners of the Rugby and District Amateur Association Football Division 3 Cup, present their trophy to the camera. Pictured are R. Hawkey (Hon. Sec.), L. Anderton, W. Louch, H. Arlidge, N. Webster, C. Worthington, A. Taylor, J. Greatrex, J. Russell, J. Osborne, C. Robinson, G. Taylor (Vice Capt.), W. Coleman (Capt.), E. Brown and H. Burman.

The 1922/23 Lawrence Sheriff School First XV pose outside the front doors of Big School. The people pictured include ? Knowles, ? Batchelor, ? Barford, ? Taylor, ? Mardling, ? Jordan, ? Coleman, J. Smith, T. Cluett, T.L. Higgs, Ward, H. Tarlin, W. Roxburgh, L. Carvell, E. Goodfellow, H.N. Parker, ? Tromans, H.F. Saw and ? Lawson.

Miss Mary Anderson came to Rugby in 1936 from Airdrie in Scotland. She started gymnastics at the age of 12 and joined the Co-op Gymnastics Club on the day she arrived in the town. It was a mixed club coached by Harry Mitchell. Mary worked at the BTH, joining their keep-fit classes and taking part in all of their recreational activities. In 1940 she married David Stewart, who was also a keen sportsman.

The BTH Keep-Fit Team at the Girls Club. The club was situated on land that has since been used to construct Russelsheim Way, which is part of the gyratory system on the west side of the town. The Keep-Fit Team gave exhibitions, demonstrated at Wembley and competed against teams that were also members of the Birmingham Union of Girls Clubs.

Mrs Mary Stewart (née Anderson), front left, who belonged to the BTH Rugby Girls' Keep-Fit Team, was chosen to be a member of the English ladies' fitness team which took part in a Nazi 'Strength Through Joy' European festival in Hamburg, Germany, in June 1938. The teams from twenty-two countries paraded in front of Hitler's deputy, Heinrich Himmler. The young ladies were asked (by Hitler) to refrain from smoking and not to use make-up; free exercises and skipping were the routines used. The ladies are pictured here at a London railway station on their return.

BTH Rugby cricket team, pictured outside what is now the GEC Social Club in Hillmorton Road, 1946.
Back row, left to right: A. Appleby, D. Bassett, W.F.R. Morgan, D.W.R. Sewell, D.J. Pitstow,
J. Murgatroyd, F. Wilson. Front row: A.E. Wilson, H. Davis, C.E. Ford (Capt.), R. Hindle, L. Dickens,
L.C.J. Carvell.

Oakfield Cricket Club team line-up, 1940: a typical English summer photograph of one of the town's
cricket club teams. It was taken some time during the first full year of the Second World War, when the
Battle of Britain was imminent if not already in progress.

BTH men's hockey 1st XI, 1947/48. Next to the umpire on the left of the back row is Jimmy Murdoch and next to him is David Stewart. It was a very successful team, playing against other works teams and teams from the universities.

The 1947 winning bowls team (BTH 'B') poses for the camera with the Finch Cup. Back row, left to right: E.R. Atkinson, J. Richardson, G. Atkins, E.H. Tafford, R.S. Allison, H. Neale, L. Burdett, H. Buswell, S. Moscrop. Front row: J. Bentley, W.R. Jackson (Capt.), J.W. Johnson.

In the 1930s Rugby was an international venue for polo, with matches taking place on Rugby School's polo fields (still called Near Polo and Far Polo) and on Lord Inchcape's field opposite his residence at Cawston House. In the photograph the Duke of Windsor, formerly Prince of Wales and King Edward VIII, is seen sitting on his pony on one of these occasions.

Linda Sutch, on *Maisie*, receives her rosette at the Rugby Pony Club's Members Only Show, summer 1956.

Children enjoy the fountain at the open-air swimming pool, which was once the mill pool at the Avon Mill, Newbold Road, 1946. The former mill house became an inn during the latter part of the nineteenth century when water abstraction from the River Avon by the Rugby Waterworks reduced the mill's capacity and consequent income. The Bagshaw family were the millers from the 1820s until 1872.

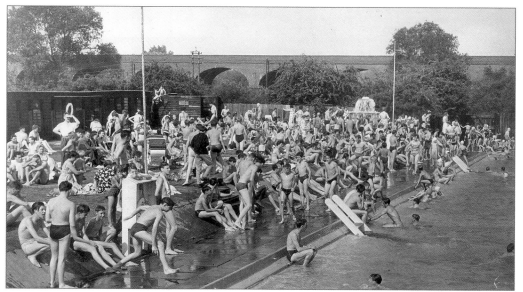

This photograph shows the location of the crowded pool more clearly, with the railway viaduct in the background. The mill (first recorded in the 1086 Domesday Survey as having a worth of 13s 4d) was closed in 1930 having been run by the Hayes family since 1884. Fred Hayes' son, Jason, took over in 1921 and his granddaughter, Emily, continued to run the Avon Mill Inn after the mill's closure. The swimming pool was opened on 13 July 1929. Mr Albert Shilvcock was Manager/Superintendent of the baths from the mid-1930s until 1949.

One way of cooling off during a hot summer in the mid-1950s for John and Jean Anderson from Scotland, who were on holiday in Rugby with his sister, Mary Stewart.

Rugby's outdoor swimming baths, 1930. Gazing at the camera are sisters Gwen Stovell and Evelyn Gwillim with Joan Stovell, aged 2.

LOOKING AT WEDDINGS

*The marriage of Clem Harrison and Edith Ellingham,
who met at a dance in St John's Hall, took place toward
the end of the Second World War, on 3 June 1944, at
St Andrew's parish church.*

On 20 June 1917 Richard Collins married
Miss Dora Silvester at Newbold-on-Avon
church. It was wartime, and not long after this
Mr Collins, having returned to the front line
in France, was taken prisoner and sent to work
in salt mines somewhere in Germany. On his
return from captivity they eventually settled in
Newbold and raised four children, three boys
and a girl, celebrating fifty years of marriage
in 1967.

The marriage of Percy Cyril Hargrave, of Braunston, and Jessica Green, of Hillmorton, 1920s. The
wedding took place in Braunston, and this photograph was taken behind the village baker's shop of Earnest
Albert Hargrave.

On 8 October 1929 Miss Elsie Watts walks up the path into St Andrew's Church on the arm of her father James Watts, with the original Lawrence Sheriff almshouse in the background. The lower photograph shows the wedding party after Elsie's marriage to James Bunyard. They are looking dispirited because the bridegroom's younger brother, aged only 16, had recently died. Mr Bunyard's mother had wanted to postpone the wedding but he objected, so his mother decreed that there would be no smiles on the photographs. Elsie worked at McKinell's Grocers in Sheep Street and when Mr McKinell found her in tears she told him that her fiancé had spent the honeymoon money on his brother's funeral. He promptly told her to dry her eyes and gave her enough money for a week in Blackpool.

Bernard J. Austin and his bride, formerly Miss Annie A. Lea, after their wedding at Cambridge Street Methodist Church on 26 May 1928, seen here with the Minister, the Revd W.B. Smith. Mr Austin, a founder member of the Rugby Brotherhood, was a music teacher by profession, and his wife was a school teacher who specialised in helping children with learning difficulties.

A Newton village wedding, St Mary's Church, Clifton, 25 October 1930. The bride and groom, Ethel Denton and Sid Addison, are pictured outside one of the council houses in Newton village. Left to right: Eddie Hancocks, Ted Addison (best man), the bride and groom, Fred Tew and Kath Grimmitt. The lady sitting down on the right is the bride's mother, Sarah Denton.

Joe Frankton junior and his bride, formerly Miss Sybil Hirons of Thurlaston, pictured in the grounds of Lion Farm, Dunchurch, after their wedding in the 1920s. Mr Frankton's brother Tom was best man and one of the matrons of honour was Mrs Borrey. The couple later ran Home Farm at Dunchurch.

Bride and groom, Audrey and Edward Smith, are caught by the camera after their Coronation year wedding at St Peter's Church, October 1953. They are crossing Clifton Road, with guests, to the Church Hall opposite where the reception was held. The hall was burnt down some years later and houses were built on the site. The Lodge Plugs sign is no longer there and the Central Railway behind remains silent.

A wartime wedding: bride and groom, Betty and Alistair Crowe, with their wedding party at St Andrew's Church on 7 September 1940. Mr and Mrs Crowe were keen members of the Rugby Scottish Society, as is their daughter Jane.

The wedding of John Littlewood and Miss Rosemary Underwood, which took place at Rugby Parish Church on 29 September 1962. The bride and groom are pictured with their parents, the bridegroom and bridesmaids. The bridesmaid on the right-hand side is Miss Ann Collins and the bride's parents, Tom and Amy Underwood, are standing next to her.

CHILDREN AT PLAY

Is she a sheriff or is she a deputy? Eighteen-month-old Heather Carter poses in her cowboy outfit in front of the wigwam in the garden of her Claremont Road home, 1961. Sister Hazel was the Red Indian and many hours of fun were enjoyed.

John Perkins, aged about 2 years, smiles at the camera from the depths of the washing basket. The photograph was taken in the family's garden in Sidney Road in about 1930. Many of the houses on the estate were newly built, hence the lack of taller trees in the background.

Teasing the back garden chickens! Elizabeth Aliberti is pictured here in the chickens' food bucket in 1948. Many people kept chickens in their gardens (mainly as a source of eggs) before, during and after the Second World War, but in the 1990s this would be a rare sight.

Ups and downs: Miss Pat Lamb and her cousin Peter Lewis ride the see-saw in Merton's Recreation Ground, *c.* 1935.

A victim of the war. Pictured enjoying himself in Caldecott Park is Hans, one of ten Polish children from a refugee camp in Hamburg, who spent ten weeks in Rugby, arriving in June 1958. Also in the picture, seated in the middle of the girls, is Gillian Cross, daughter of the family who fostered Hans for the duration of his stay.

Young Andrew Gibbs sits astride his toy dog in the family garden at Newbold-on-Avon, 1955. In the background an Anderson (air raid) shelter, converted for use as a garden shed, can be seen. These wartime relics were once a commonplace sight in gardens, but today (1997) they are rarely seen except on allotments.

Pictured on his bicycle is Roy Stovell. The elegant metal railings in Avenue Road, seen here in 1938, were destined to fall victim to the drive for raw materials for munitions when they were removed during the Second World War.

A large assembly of children and adults photographed at a children's party in the BTH canteen. The building was apparently a First World War aircraft hangar. The date of the photograph is not known, but it could be some time in the 1930s.

We're happy because it's Christmas! Lots of smiling faces at a Christmas party held for employees' children in the works canteen at Lodge Plugs, St Peter's Road, 1955. Phil Addison is sitting on the right-hand end of the third row.

Winifred and Dorothy Perkins *c.* 1900.
They were the daughters of C.W. Perkins,
builder of Hillmorton. Dorothy (Doll)
grew up to marry Tom Rate who travelled
the surrounding villages as a fishmonger.
They later became licensees of the Golden
Lion, in Regent Street, Leamington Spa,
and latterly, for many years until their
retirement, licensees of the Sheaf and
Sickle at Long Lawford.

Mrs Dorothy Beck appears here aged about
10 wheeling her bike in the 1920s. Her dress,
white with green spots, was made by two
ladies in Hillmorton village. It was made to
grow with her, having several tucks that
could be removed; she did not like it! The
photo was taken in the back yard of her house
in Hillmorton.

John Perkins, 10 years old and living in Sidney Road, poses for the camera before flying his treasured model aeroplane during the family summer holiday in Eastbourne. This was in the late 1930s, and seaside holidays were soon to be a thing of memory.

Smile for the camera! Two little girls, aged 3 and 2, produce the requested smile. Jane Thompson (on the left) and Patricia Golding are pictured at the allotments opposite the public house in Catthorpe.

Hazel Carter is seen enjoying her birthday with her sister Heather and friends in the garden of her home in Claremont Road, May 1964. All were pupils of Northlands School in Pinders Lane. The girls are, left to right: Hazel Carter, Alain Rogers, Margaret Hannah, Amanda Brace, Fiona Gibbs, Coral Townsend and Heather Carter (centre front).

Tony Hoflin stands by his bicycle in the garden of his home at 81 Murray Road, 1931. He is wearing his Lawrence Sheriff School rugby jersey.

My favourite toy! A summer day in 1935, and young Kathleen Austin stands next to her beloved golliwog in the garden of her childhood home. Manufacture of this once commonplace toy is no longer permitted.

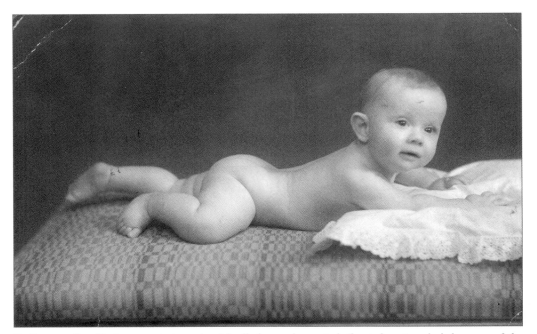

Feeling comfortable but wondering what it's all about: the typical (front down) nude baby pose of the 1930s. A very young Jim Addison is bemused by the camera in the latter part of the decade. Jim grew up in the village of Newton Biggin and now owns an engineering business in Southam Road, Dunchurch.

A happy childhood scene in spite of the war, 1943. Miss Dorothy Willis and one of her charges rake up loose straw in this rural scene.

A group of Holy Trinity Church choirboys stand on the top of the tower, *c.* 1946/7. On the left, wearing a cap, is Gordon Watts; next to him is ? Cave, then David Price. The tall boy in glasses next to David is Trevor Cox and to his left is David Colley and then ? Handwell. In front of David Price, hand on chin, is David Richards. At the extreme left of the back row is Brian Smith. The church has now been demolished.

Bernard Austin, aged about 10, is seen as proud possessor of his first drum, *c.* 1908. His mother, a widow, insisted that he first had to learn to play the piano before he could have a drum. This turned out to be a wise decision as he went on to become a well-known music teacher in the town of Rugby.

Maud Brown, aged 2, seated on her own pony,
c. 1894. She was the sister of J.T.E. Brown,
whose music shop is shown on page 119.

Fully kitted out, David Stewart, aged around 15 or
16, poses in 1930s Boy Scout uniform complete
with bugle.

Welton School May Day, 1927. Pictured from left to right in their finery are May Queen Mary Harrison and attendants Joan Cox and Clem Harrison (aged 5).

The cast of *Rumpelstiltskin* pose for the camera. This children's play was performed at Rogers Hall, Hillmorton in 1940 by a group of young people, organised by one of the mothers. Taking part were Dorothy Rossiter as the King, Mary Austin (with the mob cap), Beryl James and Kathleen Austin (courtiers). The three other girls were sisters who lived in Hillmorton, Olwyn, Sylvia and ? Pritchard.

At Catthorpe Fête, *c.* 1911. In awe of the camera, Arthur Edward, Kathleen Eva, Ethel and Sidney Wilfred Addison, of Little Biggin near Newton, pose in their fête costumes. The girls, dressed as daffodils, had been told not to put their collars outside the costume, so Kathleen Eva was in trouble when her mother saw this photograph.

SCHOOLS &
ORGANISATIONS

*Pupils of Shawell Junior School show off their newly
constructed puppets, 1952. Back row, left to right:
Linda Sutch, Richard Thompson. Third row: Marshall
Barfield, Joyce McCauley, Jane Thompson, Pauline
Bareham, Jimmy Kenny. Second row: -?-, Frank Howe,
Leslie Bastock, Adrian Wood, Pat Golding. Front row:
Sandra Barfield, Fred Clarke, Julia Knight, Penny
Sutch and Carol Harris.*

Pictures of boys and girls of Eastlands School, 1910–15. The girls and boys were accommodated in separate buildings and attended the school between the ages of 5 and 14. Among the girls is Annie Lea (second row from back, fourth from left), who later became a student teacher at the school after finishing her education at the Arnold High School (later Rugby High School for Girls) in Elsee Road. The headmistress on the left was Miss Gamble, who was still at the school into the 1930s. The other photo shows a group of prefects (senior boys) with someone who is probably the headmaster.

This photograph of St Matthew's Sunday School was taken in about 1912; it met at the vicarage in Bilton Road. Mrs Joyce Menesse (née Squires) is seated fourth from the left in the centre row; her father, Joseph Squires, was chief churchwarden at St Matthew's for many years.

Pupils of Hill School, Leamington Hastings, face the photographer, 1905/6. Marie Hicks, aged 13 or 14, and later mother of Tony Hoflin, is in the centre of the back row. Also in the picture are Marie's two brothers, Jack (in front of Marie) and Ted (just in front to the left). Ted later went to Lawrence Sheriff School in Rugby and played cricket for the school. He was unfortunately killed in 1917, aged 20, during the First World War and his name appears on the memorial tablet in Big School.

A group of St Andrew's Murray C of E Secondary Modern School pupils, May 1895. The pupils include A. Colman, ? Shepherd, ? Welsh, E. Russel, ? Gear, H. Hessian, W. Dawson, A. McLeod, R. Staines, ? Wooding, ? Meadows, R. Miller, W.J. Allan, ? Barrie, ? Moss, W. Dodd, F.J. Gibson, E. Dimblebee and W. Odey.

The taking of this photograph of Eastlands Boys School, in about 1930, appears to have been a serious business as there is hardly a smile to be seen! The headmaster, on the right of the group, is Mr Rowse.

Benn Secondary School pupils pose for the camera, 1950. The school building, seen in the background, is on the corner of Claremont and Craven Roads. No longer a school, it is currently the Benn Education Centre which comprises the Intercultural Support Centre and the Rugby Parents Centre.

Lawrence Sheriff School's Form Middle Vb, with their form-master, J.H. Lerrigo, in 1938. Those who still live in Rugby include A.P. Woods (rear row, first on left), A.P. Fletcher (back row, sixth from left), J.L. Philipps (seated, second from left) and R.C. Chapman (seated, third from left).

A group of children who attended Miss Buckler's Nursery School pictured enjoying themselves in the summer of 1961. The school was in an extended bungalow on the corner of Sidney Road and Fareham Avenue.

School during the Second World War. At Barby C of E School, Mrs A. Austin takes her class of children of mixed ages. Owing to a shortage of teachers during the war, classes were large, added to which 3-year-old children also went to school to enable their mothers to do war work. These toddlers were put to bed in canvas cots for an hour each afternoon by the teacher.

New Bilton School, 1947. Mrs A. Austin (seen opposite with her wartime class at Barby) marches her first bus-load of children through the playground for their trip to Wicksteed Park, an outing doubtless eagerly anticipated by these New Bilton youngsters.

The members of Newton Chapel Sunday School are pictured standing outside the chapel building, 1950s. Mr and Mrs Randall (far right and far left) successfully ran the Sunday school for the village children. Among them are Susan Slater, Pat Richards, Eric Collier, Joyce Fretter and Margaret Foxon.

The headmaster, Cordy Wheeler (fifth from left in front row), and assistant masters at Lawrence Sheriff School pose for the camera in 1938. Included in the second row from the back are D.V. Skeet (third from left), A. McLeish-Smith (fifth from left), A.W.K. Ingram (seventh from left), E.J. Lay (eighth from left) and J. Lewis (ninth from left). In the front row (third from left) is J. Evans. Messrs Skeet and Lewis were in their first year at the school; both eventually retired in 1974.

Pupils of Rugby High School for Girls celebrate the school's twenty-first birthday with a tea party arranged by the PTA in St Peter's Church Hall. In spite of it being wartime (1940), with consequent restrictions, sufficient food had been got together.

A group of Rugby High School pupils, 1951. The tennis courts and the rear view of the school can be seen. Ten years later the school moved to new premises in Longrood Road and the building shown here, in Clifton Road, has now been demolished and replaced by housing. A reminder of the school remains as two school house names have been given to the new streets, Brontë and Curie Close. From left to right the girls are Rosemary Underwood, Barbara Branston, Gillian Hitchcock, Denise Browning, Rosemary Cuell, Anne Cluett and Jennifer Mathias.

Four Harris School librarians pose outside the Overslade Lane school, October 1964. Left to right: Anne Parris, Julie Aliberti, Susan Valentine, Christine Woods.

The cast of Molière's *Le Bourgeois Gentilhomme*, produced by Mr Brierley at Lawrence Sheriff School in 1950. It is interesting to notice the younger pupils playing the female roles, no longer necessary with the currently combined Lawrence Sheriff and Rugby High School productions.

Pupils of Murray Boys' School are seen dressed up for their Christmas Concert, 1936. Among those taking part are Frank Gibbs, Derek Kendall, Peter Budd, Peter Ash, Billy Garrett, John Edge, Albert Steel, David Guthrie and Billy Whitfield.

The cubs of 8th Rugby (Holy Trinity) study the camera after a rounders match in Whitehall Recreation Ground in 1954. Pictured at the back is Akela Miss Harper. In the second row, David Wilkinson is second left, followed by Melvyn Wharton, Keith Howells and Robert Limb. In the front row, David Richardson is second from the right.

The Rugby School pipe band was formed in 1962, when this photograph of the Army Cadet Force Inspection Day was taken by David Stewart, who had taught the Scottish pipes to the boys at Rugby since the late 1930s. They practised in the school armoury. David was appointed honorary piper to the school.

The 1st Rugby Company of the Girls Brigade march past their Rugby Baptist Church headquarters, early 1950s. The Brigade Captain, Beryl Redfern, is seen with the colour party of Rosemary Mays, Gretta Pike and Mary Absolem. The gable end front of the old indoor swimming baths is visible in the background.

'Steadfast and sure', the 1st Rugby Company of the Boys' Brigade marches by the corner of Naseby and Cromwell Roads, early 1950s. Captain Harry Gray follows the colour party led by Reg Hurst. Gilbert Harris, John Seekings, John Morgan and Trevor Hillman with Lieutenant B. Pollard are some of the members seen on their Sunday parade.

The cast of *Sunrise Land*, a play performed by children at Long Lawford School in 1912.

A Dutch Fair at the Girls Welcome Club, 15 June 1929. Pictured second left in the front row is Evelyn Clare Brown, and second left in the second row is Maud Holman. On the far left, in the hat, is the matron of the club, who lived in a house at the side of the club in North Street. The premises have since been demolished.

Members of St George's Church Young Communicants Fellowship pick primroses after a cycle ride to Princethorpe Woods, March 1949. Several members of the group still enjoy an annual reunion. Back row, left to right: Geoff Cochrane, Brian Borton, Christopher Perkins. Front row: Kathleen Austin, Margaret Martin, Dorothy Perkins.

Pupils of Dorrie Kenyon's Dancing School proudly hold up their newly presented diplomas for the photographer, c. 1952–3. Dancing lessons were given in premises above Horace Stephens' hairdressers in Little Church Street.

TOWN & COUNTRY

Three generations of the same family take a break on the allotment, 1958. Harry Carter poses with his son Brian and granddaughter Hazel. Brian still cultivates the same plot on the Eastlands Allotments; it originally belonged to his father-in-law, Bernard Austin.

Dated 1867, this drawing shows the house that once stood on the present site of the Royal Bank of Scotland. It was originally built for the National Provincial Bank, which opened in 1867. The first branch of the bank was opened at Gloucester in 1834 and the Rugby branch was established shortly afterwards in Market Place. The old house was once a farmhouse occupied by Samuel Noon whose fields were located between Bath Street and Railway Terrace, William Street and the cattle market. He was noted for the quality of his home-brewed beer.

Church Street. This was one of the town houses pulled down to make room for the development of Regent Street.

A Salvation Army Corps was opened in Rugby in 1882, and meetings were held in the Albert Hall, Albert Street. In 1898 the meetings were held at the Citadel in Castle Street, and in 1944 the headquarters were moved to the new Citadel in Bennfield Road, which is pictured here in 1954.

This photograph of Rugby's first police station in Plowman Street, which was erected soon after 1840, was taken prior to 1906 when it was converted into houses. The second police station, also superseded and not long since demolished, was built in Railway Terrace in 1905.

The Baptist Church in Rugby has a long history. Above is a photograph of the original front of the Church in Castle Street, which later became the Brotherhood House. The opening service was held on Tuesday 27 September 1881 by the Revd J.G. Greenhough MA and the Revd James Thew (both from Leicester). The origins of Rugby Baptist Church go back to 1808, when the Church was founded by Sir Egerton and Lady Leigh, who resided at Brownsover Hall. Although Sir Egerton was a member of the Leigh family from Cheshire, he was in fact born in South Carolina, USA, in 1762, prior to Independence. The present home of the Church is in Regents Place, which was originally part of the Moat Estate. The foundation stones were laid in March 1905 and the opening ceremony took place in February 1906. The photograph below shows the interior of the old Church in Castle Street.

Cemetery Lodge in Clifton Road was the home of Charles Nash, who was cemetery keeper for many years up to the 1920s. He and his wife brought up a family of two boys and four girls here. The post of cemetery keeper no longer exists and the property is now privately owned.

Rose Mount in Lawford Road was built by Mr Atty, who lived there until 1890. The house was then occupied by the Seabrook family until 1937. On 9 March 1937 it was offered for sale, but it was later withdrawn and eventually demolished. The man on the terrace may be Mr Atty.

West Street disappeared in 1959 when Corporation Street was driven through to join Newbold Road. Quite a few shops were pulled down including Bell and Bells the chemist and Pete's fish and chip shop. The street led into West Leys on the left and Chapel Street on the right. The Queen's Head and the Forester's Arms were on the corners of West Street and West Leys. Smith's greengrocers, Bastin's sweet shop and Tommy Linley (tailor) were all in West Leys. There were a few cottages and Hall's builder's yard was in the far corner. Part of West Leys still exists and George's poultry shop was moved back, but is still there today.

This photograph of the junction of Newbold Road, Park Road and North Street was taken in 1957 just prior to the construction of Corporation Street. The old Granada (ex-Plaza) cinema is off picture on the left, and behind the trees are the Northfield offices of the borough treasurer (formerly Northfield Nursing Home). On the right are the lodge grounds of The Lawn (pictured elsewhere).

A view of Warwick Street, 1955. Mr and Mrs J. Brightwell lived at no. 7, one of a short row of cottages next to Frost the printers, Cleaver Ltd (bathroom fittings, etc.), Woolley (fish and chip shop) and a café. On the corner of Union Street there was a health food shop. All these properties were demolished to make way for the gyratory road in the early 1980s.

A picture of the site clearance in the late 1970s prior to building Rugby's first modern covered shopping mall, currently (in 1997) called Clock Towers. The view is from Corporation Street looking toward North Street, with the two towers of St Andrew's Church on the right and on its left the roof of the Rugby Tavern (formerly the Windmill). The building with the fire escape is the old Crown House, now the NatWest Bank (1997).

The Methodist Church, after which Chapel Street was named, is seen partially demolished, 1982. Chapel Street is on the right with Lennon's former shop on the corner of Drury Lane. The original entrance to the church, adjacent to the property currently occupied by Next (1997), was replaced by a shop. The Rugby Methodists were able to have a modern church built in Russelsheim Way on land made available by the gyratory development.

A photograph of the long-gone Whitehall, after which the road is named, appeared in the first *Rugby & District in Old Photographs*; however, this one is taken from a different viewpoint. The camera is in Lower Hillmorton Road with Whitehall Road to the left and Clifton Road (Lawrence Sheriff School would be behind the far left corner) directly in front. The date of the photograph is unknown.

The Lawn, Newbold Road, was, in 1852 when this illustration appeared in the *Lady's Newspaper*, a boarding school and 'Maison d'Education des Demoiselles'. Archery, an acceptable sport for ladies of that era, is in progress. In 1855 the school was moved to Waterloo Terrace (the next house) and The Lawn became a private residence from 1861 until 1937, when it was bought by Rugby Corporation and used as council offices.

Pedestrianisation of this part of the town centre began as long ago as 1969, when High Street and Sheep Street were closed to through traffic with the exception of buses and emergency vehicles. A Midland Red R86 bus exercises its right of passage across Chapel Street from Market Place just after the change was made.

Hilton's Garage in North Street (the petrol pumps are visible but the building is behind the camera) was built in 1922, and the houses facing (including Mr Benn's house on the right) were demolished in 1929.

New Bilton flour mill, erected in 1858 by the Rugby Flour and Bread Company, stood near to the Leamington railway line bridge in Lawford Road. The company, formed in 1856, was wound up in 1874 after the premises were almost destroyed by fire in the previous year.

Windsor Court, which was so named because Windsor chairs were manufactured here during the latter part of the nineteenth century.

This view of Butler's Leap in Clifton Road, of unknown date, is unrecognisable today. Now there is an industrial estate on the right with a road linking through to Boughton Road and Brownsover.

An early picture of Rugby Radio Station, which was opened in 1926 and, in 1927, operated the first long-distance radio telephone service. Twelve tall masts were erected and could be seen from miles away with their red warning lights shining at their tops. As many wires were buried underground as were strung from the tops of the masts.

I have walked over
this bridge many
times with Auntie Ivy
& my Auntie Alice
carrying on from the
right of the picture is
the Oxford & Union canal
where we walked

I remember the new
Radio Station being built
It was quite a event.

The Market Place building pictured in the process of construction in 1893 was Bennet's hairdressers. In more recent times it was an optician's and later a photograph processing shop. It is currently (1997) being used by Next, and the original frontage was revealed during this most recent renovation.

The Grand Hotel, which stood on the corner of Albert Street where Kingsforth House now stands (in 1997 the DSS Office). From 1878 until 1882 the building was a rollerskating rink after which it was converted into a hotel and opened under the name of the Rugby Private Hotel. In 1902 it was taken over, doubled in size, and renamed the Grand Hotel. It was demolished in 1975. As the Grand it was very popular for wedding receptions and other functions.

Being fleeced in the old-fashioned way: sheep shearing as it used to be done at Mr Boneham's farm near Rugby, 1920s. Mrs Boneham was the daughter of Mr and Mrs J. Frankton (see p. 78).

Threshing at Newton in 1938, in the days when corn was cut and stooked before being threshed to free the grain. Perched high up on the machine is Charles Denton senior, who was a local threshing and sawing contractor, with his grandson Maurice Addison.

Me in my Sunday best! Sid Addison poses for the camera outside Newton House on the road from Clifton in 1927. The house was owned by the Derby family who were local gentry.

The landlady, Mrs Eliza Green, making ice cream at the back of the Old Olive Bush public house at Flecknoe, 1916.

Mrs Hannah Webb is pictured sitting outside her daughter's house in Kimberley Road in the late 1930s. At that time they took in lodgers, mainly young men from the Welsh valleys who came to Rugby looking for work at BTH and Willans.

School Street, Dunchurch, 1899.

Dunchurch Square, before 1918. The Dun Cow Hotel can be seen in addition to the village cross and the stocks. The cross has a tapered shaft with an inscription stating that it was erected in 1813 as a milestone. The base probably belonged to an earlier cross.

The Old Olive Bush at Flecknoe, *c.* 1928. The landlady, Mrs Eliza Green, seen on page 72 making ice cream at the back of the pub, is pictured at the front of the pub with her daughter Alice. Over the years the building's appearance has hardly changed, and it looks much the same nearly seventy years later in 1997.

The Crown Inn, Grandborough. Note the man carrying buckets with a yoke across his shoulders — this was once a common sight in the countryside.

A street scene in Catthorpe village, *c.* 1900. The Cherry Tree public house and the post office are pictured with local children playing in the street.

The same street in Catthorpe village, but looking in the opposite direction. The Cherry Tree is on the left next door to a cottage, pulled down in the other photo. St Thomas' Church can also be seen, together with the Campbell house which is now Home Farm, farmed by Mick Grindle.

The Lutterworth Road, Pailton, 1890.

Grandma and Grandad Coleman (Agnes and Willie) by some wooden steps with their granddaughter Edith Ellingham behind them, 1927. This photograph was taken in the area of Newbold which is now Parkfield Road, running alongside the railway.

May Lane, which connects Addison Road to Bilton Road, was not smooth tarmac in 1961 as can be seen from this photograph. Local residents were urgently requesting that the surface should be made up without further delay.

A spectacular ice and snow display at Newbold Quarry, mid-1940s.

Mrs Mary Anne Nash is pictured working on
her pillow lace in the garden of her home at
Cemetery Lodge, Clifton Road, June 1909.

On this day in 1887 the whole nation
celebrated Queen Victoria's Golden Jubilee.
Mr and Mrs John Frankton were captured by
the camera, standing at the door of their home
in Thurlaston to record their part in the
celebration. He is wearing a special ribbon to
mark the occasion.

Miss Frances Birch Winstanley lived at
Burford House in Church Walk from
1876 to 1912. Her mother was the
daughter of the Revd William Birch, who
at one time ran a boarding house in the
town and later built Burford House. The
Winstanley family, whose estates were in
Braunstone near Leicester, had provided
several Leicestershire High Sheriffs over
the years.

Whitehall Recreation Ground, 1927. Gwen Stovell, on the left, and her friends smile for the camera.

Part of the interested crowd of spectators outside the Clifton Road electricity sub-station at the moment the new Mazda Mercra Street lighting was switched on by the Mayor of Rugby The result is shown below in High Street.

Pioneering ideas in electric lighting were developed and produced in Rugby by the British Thomson-Houston Company Ltd. For many years the streets in the town were used for experiments in external lighting.

WARTIME EXPERIENCES

Wartime day nursery, Holbrook Avenue, 1944–5. Pictured is Miss D. Willis ('Nursey Willie' to her small charges) who was one of the staff employed by the local authority to care for young children, from babies in prams to 5-year-olds, while their mothers were engaged in war work. They were all given their daily cod liver oil and concentrated orange juice, and they also had to endure a daily search for head lice. An afternoon rest in canvas cots was also part of the daily ritual.

On 25 June 1940 Pailton School was damaged by an enemy bomb during an air raid. The front porch is shown in this photograph.

The headmaster's house, pictured here, was badly damaged on the same occasion.

Private James Starkey of the Coldstream Guards and the officers' dog Sandy eye the camera outside Mustafa Barracks in Alexandria, 1940. Born in New Bilton, Starkey joined the army in 1939 and served in North Africa and France, transferring to the SAS and then the Military Police. He wrote war poems (see left) which were published in the *Coldstream Guards Gazette*. He was medically discharged after suffering a leg injury.

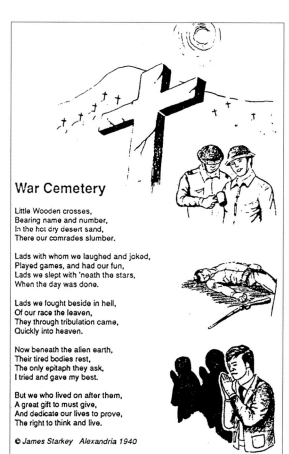

War Cemetery

Little Wooden crosses,
Bearing name and number,
In the hot dry desert sand,
There our comrades slumber.

Lads with whom we laughed and joked,
Played games, and had our fun,
Lads we slept with 'neath the stars,
When the day was done.

Lads we fought beside in hell,
Of our race the leaven,
They through tribulation came,
Quickly into heaven.

Now beneath the alien earth,
Their tired bodies rest,
The only epitaph they ask,
I tried and gave my best.

But we who lived on after them,
A great gift to must give,
And dedicate our lives to prove,
The right to think and live.

© *James Starkey   Alexandria 1940*

Almost all the metal railings in the country were removed for use in the defence industry during the early part of the Second World War. Rugby was no exception and this photo shows some being removed from the Recreation Ground in 1942. Many of the older garden walls in Rugby still have the cut-off stumps to this day.

Part of the local war effort, 1940. This photograph shows the first centimetric radar turntable for (gun)fire control ready for dispatch from British Thomson Houston's Rugby Works.

ARP (Air Raid Precautions) member Meg Hogg photographed outside ARP Headquarters in Albert Street, 1940s. The premises, known as Albert Buildings, now house the Conservative Association.

Everybody was called on to do their 'bit' during the Second World War, and many chose to work on the land. This was the case with the young lady, Miss Mary Austin, seen here in the summer of 1944. While working on a dairy farm at Barby she met her future husband who was an Italian prisoner of war. The year of publication of this book, 1997, marks their fiftieth wedding anniversary!

Battle of Britain Sunday, 1943. The parade passes Rugby's parish church (behind the camera) on Sunday 26 September. The old Lawrence Sheriff almshouses can be seen on the left. Battle of Britain Sunday was celebrated in recognition of the RAF's victory over the Luftwaffe in the English skies three years previously.

'Home Guard Sunday', 14 May 1944. The Mayor, Councillor S.P. Smart, was present at a service held in the Recreation Ground (Whitehall) to celebrate the fourth anniversary of the Home Guard (affectionately known as 'Dad's Army'). After a parade through the town the Mayor took the salute outside Lawrence Sheriff School. The photograph shows them in Warwick Street (now part of the gyratory system) with St Matthew's Church in the background.

On 2 September 1940 the hundred thousandth cup of tea was served in the free canteen provided for servicemen at Rugby station. The Mayor, Alderman R.H. Myers, the Mayoress and Miss D.S. Myers are on hand to serve the celebratory cup of tea.

A group of young men fill sand bags for air raid protection at Hillmorton, 1940. They include Archie Russell, John Herd, David Stewart and Jack Pedder, all of whom shared digs in Bath Street and worked at BTH Rugby.

Stanley Road celebrates VE Day, 8 May 1945, with a street party. Fighting continued in the Far East and VJ Day was not to come until 15 August 1945.

'Holidays at Home' celebrations are enjoyed by the crowd in Caldecott Park in 1947 during the austerity years following the end of the Second World War.

EVENTS & ENTERTAINMENT

One of the many floats decorated and paraded for the BTH Rag procession, organised by the apprentices to raise funds for the Hospital of St Cross. Mazda lamps, which the pictured float represented, were manufactured by BTH at a small factory in Lower Hillmorton Road. The date of the photograph is not known.

On 19 October 1932 there was a Charter Day procession, with many floats representing businesses and organisations in the town. The lorry illustrated here was entered by the Symington Corset factory, which was once a major employer of women in the town.

A float produced for a pre-Second World War BTH Rag aiming to raise money for the Hospital of St Cross. Joy Stovell (top row, third from left) and Dolly Stovell (top row, fourth from left) are pictured.

George V is proclaimed to succeed his father Edward VII, Rugby Market Place, 20 May 1910. The proclamation was read to the assembled citizens by Mr W. Dewar, Chairman of Rugby Urban District Council. Note the large number of firemen who are restraining the crowd.

The decorations in Hillmorton Road for Queen Victoria's Diamond Jubilee celebrations, 22 June 1897. The picture is taken looking in the direction of Whitehall Road, and on the right the far corner of Barby Lane can be seen as it was without the Temple Speech Room, which was not built until 1908/9.

In July 1961 Rugby enjoyed the company of Queen Elizabeth, the Queen Mother, when she opened the new Town Hall and the Benn Memorial Hall, where she had lunch. Earlier she had been to the BTH works (now GEC, 1997). After a short visit to Rugby School she left by helicopter from the Close. In the photograph on the left the official cars are driving past St Andrew's Church, while below (in characteristic hat) the Queen Mother chats to some of the crowd of well-wishers at the BTH. Pictured third left is Betty Richardson with friends, including Kath Stanyon.

A photograph of North Street, taken from the corner of Windmill Lane looking toward Caldecott Park, showing the decorations for the visit of King Edward VII, 3 July 1909. This was the opening of the Temple Speech Room at Rugby School.

When the Duchess of York (now the Queen Mother) visited Rugby in 1929 to open the new out-patients' department at St Cross Hospital, an ox was donated by the Rugby and District Butchers' Association. On the far right is Read William Elliott who owned a butcher's shop at 38 Lawford Road.

In 1937 King George VI was crowned after the abdication of his elder brother Edward VIII. Once again the town was made festive for this major national event, and the photo shows decorations being put in place in Whitehall Road.

A picture of the residents of Langton Road who organised a party to celebrate the Coronation of Queen Elizabeth II, 1953. The event took place on the Lawrence Sheriff School sports field, where this photograph was taken. Among those present were Ernest and Connie Craven, who owned a general store at 29 Langton Road.

This photograph, taken in March 1936, pictures the Rugby Amateur Operatic Society production of *The Arcadians*. These musicals were an annual treat for the people of Rugby, but were hard work for the participants with rehearsals starting in March for an October production. Left to right: Archie Russell, Maurice Tallon, Brenda Stevenson, Herbert Robinson, Peggy Clipstone, William Hackliffe, Hilda Main and William Henson.

A rehearsal for the Warwickshire Coronation Pageant taking place in the grounds of Rugby Technical College, to celebrate the Coronation of Queen Elizabeth II, 1953.

Two principals and the men's chorus of the Rugby Amateur Operatic Society in their 1939 performance of the popular musical *Goodnight Vienna*. The society was founded at the end of 1919 for 'the study and production of operatic works in aid of charitable and other objectives' with an inaugural production of *Les Cloches de Corneville* in 1920. In the chorus, from left, Heber Bissell is second, John Herd is sixth, David Stewart is eighth and Neil Neville is ninth.

The Red Shadow and the Foreign Legion. Packing the stage, with the orchestra standing in front, is the full cast of the BTH Amateur Operatic and Dramatic Society production of *Desert Song*, staged at the Co-operative Hall in December 1938. This works-based group was founded in 1912, staging many Gilbert and Sullivan productions in the early days. Members were connected directly or indirectly with BTH.

Charter Day, 12 October 1932. Rugby's High Street is lined with townspeople waiting to see the procession pass through on this momentous day in the history of the town.

A dancing bear provides an unusual street scene outside Rugby School by the entrance to St Matthew's Street. The picture is believed to have been taken early this century. The bear was being used as an advertisement for a circus appearing in the town at the time.

Miss Dorothy Willis, a member of the cast, stands outside her home at 28 Ashlawn Road with a billboard advertising the Guildhouse Players' forthcoming production of *The Happiest Days of Your Life*.

A celebration dinner at the Percival Guildhouse, *c.* 1951. Mrs Betty Aspinall, middle of the front row, is seen with other members of the Guildhouse Players.

Piping in the haggis. The Rugby Scottish Society's annual Burns Night Dinner was traditionally held at the Grand Hotel, which used to be in Albert Street. The chef holds the haggis aloft while Jim Lothian has the pipes in this picture of the celebration on 25 January 1950, when David Stewart (who usually played the pipes) was President of the Society.

A dancing team from Rugby Scottish Society display their skills for the elderly residents of Bilton House, late 1950s. Among the dancers are Alistair Crowe, Janet Spence, Ian Philips and Shirley Templeton.

Restoration of the west tower of St Andrew's Church together with the five bells, 1929. This photo shows the bells and, from left to right, two workmen, C.E. Pearce, J.T. Warr, Mr Woods, Mr Cooper, Mr Beck and Mrs Beck.

An inspection by staff of Rugby Corporation, 1930s. The late Mr B.A. Hitchcock, Deputy Borough Surveyor, can be seen on the far right.

SECTION NINE

WORKERS & BUSINESSES

One of the 0–6–0 tank locos which were employed in the construction of the Great Central Railway at the end of the nineteenth century. Both this one and Annie, pictured on the next page, did not have the luxury of Barry's enclosed cab (also on the next page).

Annie was one of the locomotives used by the contractors building the Rugby section of the Great Central Railway between 1896 and 1898. Her tipping gang are seen having a welcome rest from their labours.

The locomotive *Barry* near the yard at Willoughby during construction of the Great Central Railway.

The new Great Central station, Rugby's other station, was completed in 1899, and the first passenger train to stop there was one that picked up guests for the official opening of the line at Marylebone on 9 March 1899. This photo, taken in 1900, shows the up line platform.

The old Great Central station was finally demolished on 10 June 1970. The ensuing chaos, viewed from the bridge in Hillmorton Road, brought tears to the eyes of local rail enthusiasts.

Rugby British Rail Maintenance Gang, Alf Aliberti, Peter Wilkinson, Charley Warr, Harry Golding and Bill House seen here some time in the period 1958 to 1960 with two men from Northampton. They are examining a 6 ton overhead travelling crane used for lifting the rails.

LMS railway engine cleaners, 1939. From left to right: Reg Andrews, Clem Harrison and ? Ashley. Clem Harrison was 17 at the time, having left school a year earlier to work in the payroll office. At the outbreak of war Clem was too young for military service so he joined the footplate men to progress via cleaner and fireman to become a driver. He took the first train (containing army personnel, including bomb disposal experts) from Rugby to Coventry after the notorious air raid in November 1940.

William Thomas Perkins poses by his father's builder's lorry in the yard at Hillmorton in about 1920. He was keen on shooting but, though he appears to be suitably dressed for the part, there is no sign of a gun.

This group of ladies (seamstresses) were photographed in about 1895. Three sisters of the Thomas family worked there. They are Alice, Eliza (back row, second from right), Florence (middle row, third from left) and Ada Mary Ann (front row, third from left).

The staff and workforce of the BTH Testing Department pose for the camera, 1911. Note the large motors at each side of the group. Among the group is Mr W.F. Hoflin, father of Tony Hoflin who supplied the photograph.

On 13 July 1933 the new wing of the Rugby Steam Laundry Co. Ltd was opened by the Mayor of Rugby, Alderman J.J. McKinell JP. From left to right: L.M. Crockett, Miss McKinell, the Mayor, Miss Ivy Robinson (whose married name was Burdett and who was involved with the ironing for the 'polo set' and Coton House), Miss J.M. Fenwick (the owner of the laundry) and Colonel John Brown.

Coronation celebrations, 1953. The workers in the ceramic shop at Lodge Plugs (in St Peter's Road) celebrate with Union Jacks and bunting. Sid Addison is on the right at the very back and Lil Hopcroft is on the right of the front row.

No question about the time the shutter clicked, but the year cannot be defined better than some time in the 1940s. The domestic staff at Newton House, Newton, stand before the camera. Ethel Addison (third from the left) was a general servant for the Derby family who owned the house.

The fitting staff at the old Rugby Gas Works, 1929. Left to right: T. Cashmore, R. Norgate, G.E. Huckle, J. Smith, J. Cashmore, J. Ingram, F. Addison.

Over's staff outing to the Cotswolds, 1949.

A group of men who worked for A.E. Frost, printers, pictured on the annual outing to Shawell, August 1913. Mr H. Moore, seen standing at the back by the tree, started at Frost's in 1907 and, except for the First World War period, worked for the company for fifty-seven years. At the rear on the right are Mr Pope and Mr Marsden. Outings were an annual occurrence for small businesses in the town – sometimes to the seaside and sometimes to the countryside and well-known beauty spots.

BTH publicity department, *c*. 1950. Included in the picture are T.M. McClellan, A. Campbell, Tony Moody, Miss Smith, Miss Hunt, Tony Hoflin, Mr Thomas, Mr Alderson, S.S. Bagshaw, Mr Hardman, Mr Bilson, Mr Page, C.H. Chaplain (manager), Mr Langley, Holly Taylor and Miss Clipstone.

One of the first GPO vans is pictured in the early 1930s with driver Thomas Gibbs standing alongside, while out delivering in Moreton Pinkney.

Reg Lewis, instructor with the ACE Driving School, poses by his car in 1952.

Members of Co-op Check Office waiting their turn to take part in their event at the Co-op Sports Day, 1944. The sports were held in Bilton Road where the Co-op funeral business property is today. Among those in the picture are Jean and Beryl Tomilia, Joyce Kidd, Grace Wakenell, Joyce Beech, Lillian King, Barbara Smith, Doreen Riddy, Edna Kidd (Joyce's sister), Mildred Tapp, Sylvia Tranter, Betty Palmer, Marie Brand, Audrey Kitchener, Rose Allen, Audrey Robbins, Sheila Gardener and Check Office supervisor Mrs Winifred Penn, seated by the airmen.

The building of one of many houses on the
Hillmorton Paddox estate by C.W. Perkins in
the 1930s. Mr Perkins began his business at
Rose Villa next to Hillmorton Village School.
He acquired the land for his yard in Dunsmore
Avenue (seen in the lower picture) in 1912
together with building land on the estate. The
business was taken over on his death in 1931 by
his sons Christopher John and William Thomas
(pictured with a workman), who continued to
run it until their retirement in 1965. The
premises now belong to his grandson who
trades as Christopher Charles Antiques.

Edward Hall Speight, one of the town's first photographers, was born in Westmorland in 1835 and came to Rugby in June 1861 on his appointment as headmaster of the Wesleyan School. During later years he took up photography as a hobby and in 1874 he resigned to commence business as a photographer in Dunchurch Road, where all six of his sons eventually joined the business. He died in 1919 aged 83.

Rugby Shopping Week was held at the Benn Memorial Hall in the early 1970s. In the photograph are Aileen and Bill Membery with their son William and daughter Gillian. Bill Membery managed the Army and Navy Stores in North Street, owned by his father since 1929, until it closed in the late 1970s.

Mrs Katherine M.R. Norris (née Eyre) stands outside the greengrocer's shop, (no. 287) on the corner of Hillmorton Road and Shenstone Avenue, at its opening in July 1930. Mrs Norris' brother supplied fresh fruit and vegetables direct from Wisbech in Cambridgeshire. In 1997 the shop is still there but is now a pet shop.

Mr W. Reading, who lived at Bilton, was a hedge
cutter by trade. This photograph was taken in
1875.

Cross Street butcher and game dealer. The date is not known but the dress style suggests a turn-of-the-
century date. The girls' dresses also suggest summertime so it is to be hoped that turnover of the
plenteous supply of suspended ducks, chickens and rabbits was suitably rapid.

The Dun Cow, Lawford Road. This is first mentioned as the Dun Cow in the Rugby Directory of 1871, and so it continued until the last entry as such in 1917, with a Mr J. Harris as proprietor. In 1922 it became the Workers' Union Club. The decorative heads on the columns each side of the doors can still be seen today.

Mr W.G. Silvester owned a greengrocery business on Bilton Road, on the present site of Bernhards Garden Centre. His greengrocery produce (much of which he grew himself) was delivered round the streets of Rugby by Mr C.J. Collins. The business was eventually sold to Mr E. Robinson, butcher, who later sold it on to Mr G. Bernhard.

Windmill Lane, early 1900s. The grandfather of Mrs E. Collins, George Moore, worked for Burton's lemonade factory in Windmill Lane. He is seen here standing by his dray, which was used to deliver lemonade to the villages round about. He and his wife lived in Russell Street and she was Mr Burton's housekeeper.

Rounds Bus Service of Long Lawford sold out to Midland Red in 1923. The car pictured behind the bus is a 1923 Standard Four Model Tourer.

One of Rugby's early music shops, J.T.E. Brown, Music Merchant, was situated in Albert Street and, as can be seen from the sign, catered for the whole range of music requirements from 'do it yourself' to 'sit and listen'.

J.T.E. Brown's Radio Exhibition was held at the Central Hall in Henry Street in 1938. This building, which was for a short time in the early 1930s a rollerskating rink, has undergone many alterations since this photo was taken. Now owned by Rugby Theatre and used for rehearsals and storage, it also houses the theatre bar.

A photograph of the ground floor interior of Over's bookshop when it was located in Market Place, in the present position of the Clock Tower shopping mall entrance. The windows above are more or less as they were when they were part of the first floor of the shop, but they are now only a façade. Over's moved to smaller premises in High Street to make way for the shopping mall in the late 1970s, later being bought out and becoming Hunt's bookshop, which subsequently moved across the road into the old gas showroom.

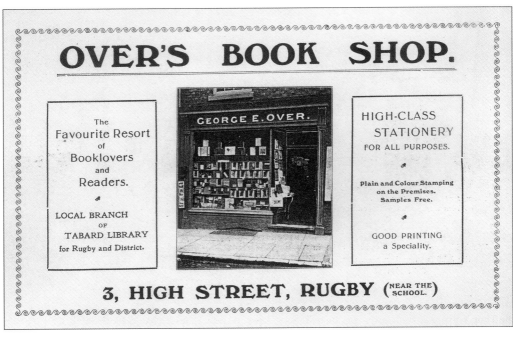

Inside the Cherry Tree public house in Catthorpe in 1968 are the licensees, Dickie and Glad Thompson, who ran the pub for thirty-nine years from 1946 to 1985. The admired small boy is their grandson, Paul Addison. Harold Johnson, gardener at Catthorpe Manor, looks on across the bar counter.

The off-licence in James Street, late 1950s. The two little girls are Susan and Pamela Lewis, daughters of the shop's proprietors, Peter and Jean Lewis. James Street is now closed to through traffic after development for housing in the area.

Woodcock's Paddox Bakery's electric bread delivery van parked opposite their bakery in Dunsmore Avenue, early 1930s. This delivery mode was way ahead of its time; most other bakers were using a horse and cart to bring us our daily bread. The sign writing on the van was carried out by William Thomas Perkins, son of builder C.W. Perkins who built (in about 1914) and lived in the house (next to his builder's yard) in the background of the photo.

Nathan's Hardware Store in Lawrence Sheriff Street, June 1959. Left to right: Mary Taylor (assistant), Tom Mason (manager) and Jean Steel (assistant).

Top Picture P.123

Have walked along
that stretch of road
with A. Ivy & A Alice
gong to Dunchurch
to see the Stuffs.

This undated picture shows a very large load turning out of Sheep Street into Lawrence Sheriff Street and thence into Dunchurch Road. The Star Inn, demolished when the gyratory road system was built, can be seen in the background on the corner of St Matthew's Street. The load, which the signboard says is a stator (possibly for a generator), would have come from the BTH Works.

At one time this was a not altogether unusual sight in Rugby. A massive transformer makes its slow progress from the BTH factory through Market Place in the spring of 1956. Corporation Street was not built in those days and these loads had to negotiate the town centre roads.

William Satchell (1801–84) and a Mr Lockington built many of the large houses in Warwick Street, Bilton Road and Hillmorton Road to meet the demand from the gentry. They had Rugby residences to enable their sons to be educated at Rugby School during Dr Arnold's time as headmaster. The properties were known as 'nabob's houses' as many of the owners were based in India. It is said that the designs owed something to similar properties in Leamington Spa which were apparently studied by the builders. William Satchell also owned Hillmorton Brick Works, which he inherited from his father, and was responsible for much of the town's original drainage system.

As stated at the beginning of this book, J. Gilbert were well known for manufacturing rugby balls. However, they started business in High Street, Rugby, as boot and shoe makers, moving in 1842 to St Matthew's Street where they carried on their business of making footwear together with the manufacture of rugby balls.

ACKNOWLEDGEMENTS

We would like to thank the following people for allowing us to use their photographs and for sharing their memories:

Jane and David Addison, Dorothy Beck, Mrs W. Brightwell, Neville Bryan, Miss B. Bunyard, R.A. Burdett, R.C. Chapman, Betty Collins, Hilda Cook, Connie Craven, Betty Cross, the late Mrs Alice Davies, Mrs D. Denham, Evelyn Clare Dickins, Mrs P. Evans, David Florendine, Mr and Mrs L. Goodway, Joanna Grindle (Senior Librarian), May Hand, Edith Harrison, Hugh Harrison, Joyce Higgs, Hugh A.W. Hoflin, James Gilbert Rugby Football Museum, Pete Lewis, Rosemary Littlewood, Aileen Membery, Mrs Joyce Menesse, Christopher Perkins, John L. Philipps, David Price, David Richardson, Stan Richardson, Mrs J. Roberts, Rugby Baptist Church, Mrs Joyce Russell, Mrs B.M. Salter (daughter of the late Mrs Norris), Brian Shilvock, Mary Stewart, Penny Sutch, Ken Taylor, Dickie and Glad Thompson, K.T. Timson, Ken and Joy Tomalin, John Twells, J. Wright.

Members of the Rugby Local History Research Group:

Mary Aliberti, Kathleen Carter, Janet Courtney, Christopher Hicks, Gywn Edwards, Dorothy Hindle, Dennis Keen, Gill Keen, John Perkins, Elizabeth Robinson, Linda Robinson, Dave Sutch, Barbara Witt and Anne Woolliscroft. A special mention must be made to Mary (Group Leader), Elizabeth, Dennis and Janet, without whose tireless efforts the book would not have been possible.

BRITAIN IN OLD PHOTOGRAPHS

Lincoln
Lincoln Cathedral
The Lincolnshire Coast
Liverpool
Around Llandudno
Around Lochaber
Theatrical London
Around Louth
The Lower Fal Estuary
Lowestoft
Luton
Lympne Airfield
Lytham St Annes
Maidenhead
Around Maidenhead
Around Malvern
Manchester
Manchester Road & Rail
Mansfield
Marlborough: A Second Selection
Marylebone & Paddington
Around Matlock
Melton Mowbray
Around Melksham
The Mendips
Merton & Morden
Middlesbrough
Midsomer Norton & Radstock
Around Mildenhall
Milton Keynes
Minehead
Monmouth & the River Wye
The Nadder Valley
Newark
Around Newark
Newbury
Newport, Isle of Wight
The Norfolk Broads
Norfolk at War
North Fylde
North Lambeth
North Walsham & District
Northallerton
Northampton
Around Norwich
Nottingham 1944–74
The Changing Face of Nottingham
Victorian Nottingham
Nottingham Yesterday & Today
Nuneaton
Around Oakham
Ormskirk & District
Otley & District
Oxford: The University
Oxford Yesterday & Today
Oxfordshire Railways: A Second
   Selection
Oxfordshire at School
Around Padstow
Pattingham & Wombourne

Penwith
Penzance & Newlyn
Around Pershore
Around Plymouth
Poole
Portsmouth
Poulton-le-Fylde
Preston
Prestwich
Pudsey
Radcliffe
RAF Chivenor
RAF Cosford
RAF Hawkinge
RAF Manston
RAF Manston: A Second Selection
RAF St Mawgan
RAF Tangmere
Ramsgate & Thanet Life
Reading
Reading: A Second Selection
Redditch & the Needle District
Redditch: A Second Selection
Richmond, Surrey
Rickmansworth
Around Ripley
The River Soar
Romney Marsh
Romney Marsh: A Second
   Selection
Rossendale
Around Rotherham
Rugby
Around Rugeley
Ruislip
Around Ryde
St Albans
St Andrews
Salford
Salisbury
Salisbury: A Second Selection
Salisbury: A Third Selection
Around Salisbury
Sandhurst & Crowthorne
Sandown & Shanklin
Sandwich
Scarborough
Scunthorpe
Seaton, Lyme Regis & Axminster
Around Seaton & Sidmouth
Sedgley & District
The Severn Vale
Sherwood Forest
Shrewsbury
Shrewsbury: A Second Selection
Shropshire Railways
Skegness
Around Skegness
Skipton & the Dales
Around Slough

Smethwick
Somerton & Langport
Southampton
Southend-on-Sea
Southport
Southwark
Southwell
Southwold to Aldeburgh
Stafford
Around Stafford
Staffordshire Railways
Around Staveley
Stepney
Stevenage
The History of Stilton Cheese
Stoke-on-Trent
Stoke Newington
Stonehouse to Painswick
Around Stony Stratford
Around Stony Stratford: A Second
   Selection
Stowmarket
Streatham
Stroud & the Five Valleys
Stroud & the Five Valleys: A
   Second Selection
Stroud's Golden Valley
The Stroudwater and Thames &
   Severn Canals
The Stroudwater and Thames &
   Severn Canals: A Second
   Selection
Suffolk at Work
Suffolk at Work: A Second
   Selection
The Heart of Suffolk
Sunderland
Sutton
Swansea
Swindon: A Third Selection
Swindon: A Fifth Selection
Around Tamworth
Taunton
Around Taunton
Teesdale
Teesdale: A Second Selection
Tenbury Wells
Around Tettenhall & Codshall
Tewkesbury & the Vale of
   Gloucester
Thame to Watlington
Around Thatcham
Around Thirsk
Thornbury to Berkeley
Tipton
Around Tonbridge
Trowbridge
Around Truro
TT Races
Tunbridge Wells

Tunbridge Wells: A Second
   Selection
Twickenham
Uley, Dursley & Cam
The Upper Fal
The Upper Tywi Valley
Uxbridge, Hillingdon & Cowley
The Vale of Belvoir
The Vale of Conway
Ventnor
Wakefield
Wallingford
Walsall
Waltham Abbey
Wandsworth at War
Wantage, Faringdon & the Vale
   Villages
Around Warwick
Weardale
Weardale: A Second Selection
Wednesbury
Wells
Welshpool
West Bromwich
West Wight
Weston-super-Mare
Around Weston-super-Mare
Weymouth & Portland
Around Wheatley
Around Whetstone
Whitchurch to Market Drayton
Around Whitstable
Wigton & the Solway Plain
Willesden
Around Wilton
Wimbledon
Around Windsor
Wingham, Addisham &
   Littlebourne
Wisbech
Witham & District
Witney
Around Witney
The Witney District
Wokingham
Around Woodbridge
Around Woodstock
Woolwich
Woolwich Royal Arsenal
Around Wootton Bassett,
   Cricklade & Purton
Worcester
Worcester in a Day
Around Worcester
Worcestershire at Work
Around Worthing
Wotton-under-Edge to Chipping
   Sodbury
Wymondham & Attleborough
The Yorkshire Wolds

To order any of these titles please telephone our distributor, Littlehampton Book Services on 01903 721596
For a catalogue of these and our other titles please ring Regina Schinner on 01453 731114